MANES AND TAILS

by

Valerie Watson

Illustrations by

Carole Vincer

KENILWORTH PRESS

First published in Great Britain by
Threshold Books, The Kenilworth Press Limited
Addington, Buckingham, MK18 2JR

Reprinted 1987, 1988, 1990 (twice), 1991, 1992, 1993 (twice)

© Threshold Books Ltd 1986

British Library Cataloguing in Publication Data
Watson, Valerie
   Manes and tails.–(Threshold picture guides).
   1.Horses–Grooming 2. Horses–Showing
   I. Title
   636.1'0833   SF285.7
   ISBN 0-901366-32-3

Typeset by Falcon Graphic Art Ltd
Wallington, Surrey, U.K.
Printed in England
by Westway Offset

CONTENTS

Introduction

Nature gave ponies manes and tails to protect them. In summer the forelock protects the eyes from flies; the mane and tail protect the rest of the body. In winter the mane becomes very greasy, which makes it waterproof and protects the animal from wind and rain. A large bushy tail protects the rear of the pony as he turns his hindquarters to the wind.

Long, flowing manes and tails can look most attractive when they are well brushed out and cared for, but they are difficult to keep in good condition, especially when the pony is living out of doors. Manes and tails often get rubbed on fences and when the pony rolls. Some of the long tail hairs will be pulled out when swished against hedges and fences. Long manes sometimes get in the way of the reins when you are riding, and do not really create a workmanlike picture in the show ring or hunting field. So if you want to perform in public with a well turned-out pony, tidying up his mane and tail will make a lot of difference. If it is done in moderation, as described in this book, the pony will look smart and will come to no harm.

Manes and tails should be brushed as part of routine grooming and before pulling or plaiting. Use a body brush, or if the hair is very coarse, an old, well-worn dandy brush. Manes and tails can be washed, but unless the weather is warm wash only the bottom part of the tail, up to the dock. Ask an experienced person to help if you and your pony are new to the task, because some ponies are quite alarmed when they feel water round their dock or dripping from the end of their tail.

Obviously there are many ways of plaiting and pulling manes and tails, but we have chosen methods which we hope will be easy for readers with small hands.

We hope that in using the book you will be successful in your efforts and will enjoy improving the look of your pony. Don't be too despondent if the first result is not a huge success. The more you practise the better you will be.

Cutting a bridle path

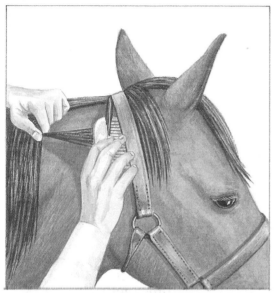

1. Separate the piece of mane to be cut by making two straight partings – about 2ins (5cms) apart – just behind the ears where the headpiece of the bridle will lie.

2. With the forelock combed forward, and using your comb to fix the mane back, check that the path will be in the right place. Then cut the piece of mane.

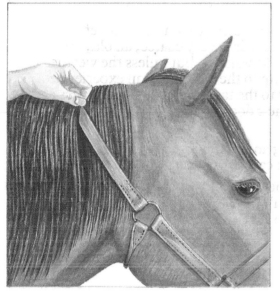

3. Keep on until you have cut the piece of mane very short and flat. The bridle path should look the same as if it had been clipped with a machine.

4. The headpiece will now lie flat and comfortably between the forelock and the mane, giving a neat appearance.

Pulling a mane

'Pulling' is a way of thinning and shortening a long thick mane in order to make it tidier, more manageable and easier to plait. However, remember that the mane protects the pony from flies in summer and from wind and rain in winter. So if your pony lives out of doors all year round, be sure to leave the mane long enough to protect him (approximately 15cms or 6ins).

Pulling involves plucking strands of hair out of the mane. On a thick mane this can take quite a long time. The hairs of the mane pull out more easily when the pony is warm and when the pores of the skin are open. Therefore, pulling the mane on a warm day or after exercise will be easier for you and more comfortable for your pony.

Using the method shown, work on the mane in small bunches, from the poll to the withers. Diagram 1 shows how to start on the first bunch by the poll. The following stages are shown on bunches further down the neck, so that you can see how the finished section should look. Try to pull out more hairs from the underside of the mane, as this will encourage the mane to lie flat. Finally, pluck out any unlevel hairs without using your comb, a few hairs at a time.

If the mane is very thick, or if your pony finds pulling an uncomfortable exercise, do not try to complete your task on one day, but take several days, working a little at a time to prevent soreness. Don't be tempted to use scissors to save time and trouble. The results are always poor. However, if your pony finds pulling completely unacceptable, tidy the mane with the help of a thinning comb.

To pull the forelock, follow the same method, making sure that the finished mane and forelock are of the same length.

BEFORE

AFTER

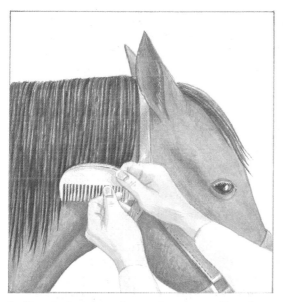

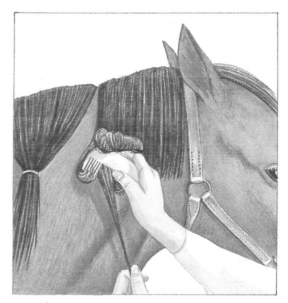

1. Brush then comb out the mane. Starting at the poll, comb a narrow bunch of mane almost all the way down. With your left hand grasp the longest hairs below the comb.

2. Holding the longest hairs firmly, backcomb the section of mane. A rubber band will keep the rest of the mane out of the way.

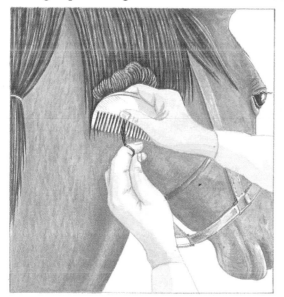

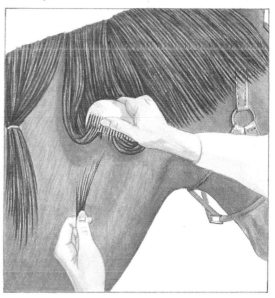

3. Wrap the longest hairs around your forefinger, ready to be pulled out. It is usual to pull out more hairs from the underside of the mane than from the top.

4. Pluck out the hairs with one brisk pull, perhaps using the comb to help. Comb out, and repeat until the bunch is short and thin enough. Continue down the mane.

Plaiting a mane

Plaiting (braiding) the mane involves dividing the hairs into bunches. Each bunch is plaited, folded under, and fastened so that it lies in a small, neat plait close to the crest. This makes the pony look smart and tidy, enhances his appearance in the show ring, and keeps the mane out of the way when jumping or hunting. It is correct to 'plait up' for most public occasions. If the mane is plaited, the tail should either be pulled or plaited, to complete the picture. Note, however, that for some specialist breed classes, such as show classes for Arabs or mountain and moorland ponies, it is incorrect to plait up. If your pony has an unruly mane, which lies on both sides of the neck, train it to lie neatly on one side by brushing it, damping it and dividing it into bunches secured with rubber bands. Remove the rubber bands at night.

When you are learning, it might take you up to an hour to plait up. Experts take about fifteen minutes.

Secrets of good plaiting:
1   It is easier to plait a mane which has been pulled. Thick manes result in chunky, cricket-ball-type plaits.
2   Brush the mane out thoroughly, then 'lay' it with a water brush. Make sure that each bunch is damp before you start to plait it: wet hair is easier to control, especially if your pony has a fine mane. Some people even use setting lotion to keep down the small hairs at the top of the crest.
3   Use your comb to make straight partings between each bunch. This creates a crisp appearance.
4   Try to make your plaiting fairly tight, especially at the top of the plait. If the plaiting is loose, the finished plait may be floppy, it may look untidy, and it may 'drop out'.
5   Normally each plait will be the same size. Divide the mane into 7, 9 or 11 bunches because, traditionally, the forelock completes the even number. Most people use their comb or a ruler to ensure that the width of each bunch is roughly the same.

A well turned-out, plaited pony is a pleasure to see. Tidy plaits can make the plainest of animals look special.

It is possible to improve your pony's looks with clever plaiting. For example, lots of little plaits will make his neck look longer, and if he has a very short neck will improve his appearance.

If the pony has a very long neck, fewer plaits will draw attention away from the length.

The appearance of a 'ewe-necked' pony may be improved by making the plaits in the dip considerably bigger than the remainder of the plaits.

Conversely, a pony with a huge crest will look better with very small plaits at the widest part of the crest.

Plaiting your pony up the night before a special occasion may be risky. It may be uncomfortable for the pony, and itchy or cheeky ponies may rub the plaits out during the night, leaving you with an awful mess to patch up in the morning, and sometimes a ruined mane.

The illustrations show two methods of plaiting: one with needle and cotton, the other with rubber bands.

If the plaits are to stay in all day, they will be more secure if they are sewn.

Rubber bands are useful for fastening up short-term plaits, when you are in a hurry. It is possible to use one rubber band for each plait, but they are more secure if you use two.

In either method the cotton or rubber bands used should match the colour of the pony's mane and should not be seen; the best plaits are those which look as though they are staying up by magic.

Plaiting a mane USING NEEDLE AND COTTON

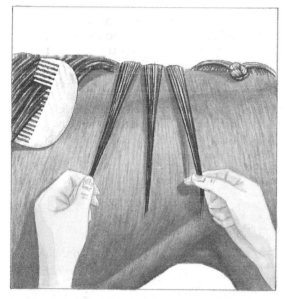

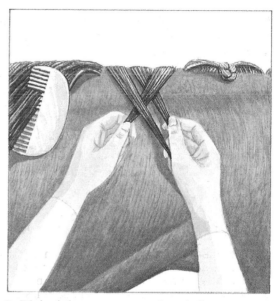

1. Here the first bunch has been plaited and the second bunch prepared. Dampen the bunch and divide it into three, making straight partings with your comb.

2. Plait right over centre then left over centre, and so on, to the end of the bunch. Plait tightly to ensure neat, secure, plaits.

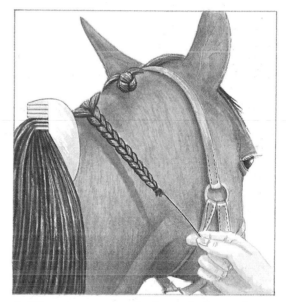

3. Hold the end of the plait firmly. Secure it by sewing through the end of the plait, wrapping the thread (knotted at the end) round it and sewing through again.

4. Then turn under the loose hairs at the end. Sew round and through, as before, until you have made a tidy end, firmly secured with thread.

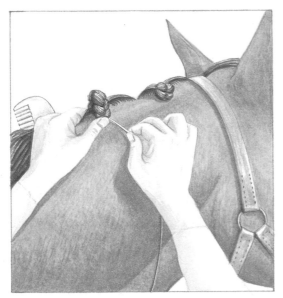

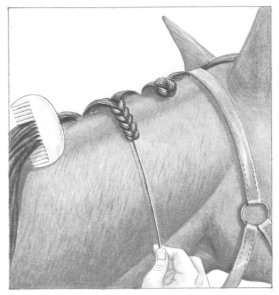

5. Double the plait under, and tuck it into the top of the neck. Sew up and down several times to secure it, taking care not to prick the pony's neck.

6. The plait should now lie down on the neck. Next, either fold or roll it up, making it short, neat, and close to the crest.

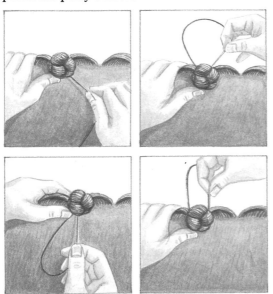

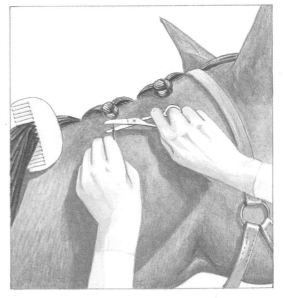

7. Now in its final stage, the plait must be securely sewn. Follow the method shown, and repeat it several times, sewing in any untidy hairs.

8. Sew neatly, showing as little thread as possible. Finish with the needle facing down, and cut the thread close to the plait.

Plaiting a mane USING RUBBER BANDS

1. Follow the method shown on page 9, but instead of using thread, wind a rubber band round the end of the plait to secure it. Keep some slack in the band.

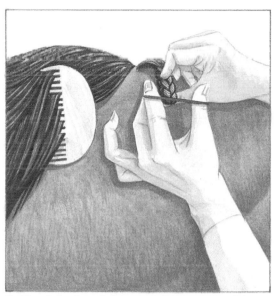

2. Double the plait up and secure it with the slack part of the band. Until you have had enough practice you will find that a *long* rubber band is easier to use.

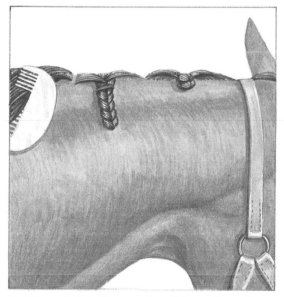

3. This plait is fastened and is ready to be doubled up or rolled into a neat plait close to the crest. The rubber bands should match the pony's mane.

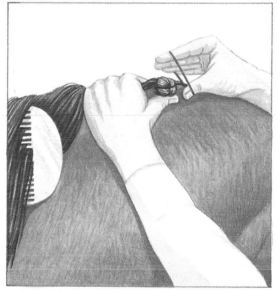

4. Double the plait up again, or roll it up into a neat ball. Take a second rubber band and fasten it around the entire plait as many times as possible.

Remedial plaiting

This pony has a ewe neck. The lower part of the neck is bulky and the crest undeveloped. Larger plaits in the dip will make the neck look a better shape.

Divide the mane into 7, 9 or 11 bunches using rubber bands. Make the bunches larger where the neck looks weak. Then plait each bunch in the usual way.

This pony has a bull neck. The crest is too big, giving a coarse appearance. If the pony has a thick mane the fault looks even worse.

Divide the mane into small bunches, making those at the thickest part of the crest smaller still. Plait as usual. The neck will then look finer.

Hogging a mane

Hogging (roaching) is the term used for clipping off all of the pony's mane and forelock.

Advantages:

1   The neck always looks tidy and there will be no mane to get in the way of your hands when you are riding.

2   Some ponies continually rub their manes if they have an irritating skin condition, such as sweet itch. The veterinary surgeon will advise treatment, but the mane may already be too short to plait. Hogging will make it neat, and in the future it will grow level.

Disadvantages:

1   You will have to buy, hire or borrow a clipping machine.

2   Your pony may be reluctant to stand still with his head down, so you will need expert help unless he is very quiet and used to being hogged.

3   A hogged mane provides no protection for the pony. Hogged ponies MUST have access to shelter from the weather and from flies.

4   The mane grows quickly and will need rehogging at least once a month.

5   Hogging is best suited to the heavier, cob-type pony with a thick neck. It makes a weak neck look more obvious.

6   If you decide to re-grow the mane, it will grow straight up on end, as though your pony has had a nasty shock! Also, the mane will not lie correctly, nor will you be able to plait it for several months.

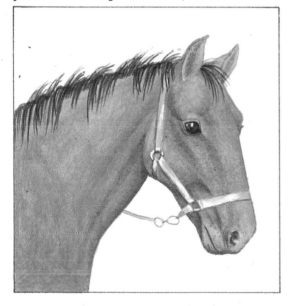

BEFORE

AFTER

1. Ask an experienced helper to hold the pony. Make sure that the clippers are clean, oiled, and working correctly. Then begin clipping slowly up the centre of the crest.

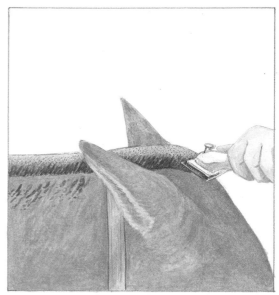

2. Stop by the poll. The pony should be taught to stand with his neck stretched out and down. Clip the forelock against the way the hair grows.

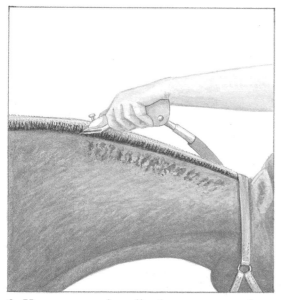

3. You may need to clip the crest towards the withers, depending on which way the hair grows. Clip both sides of the crest, taking care not to clip into the coat.

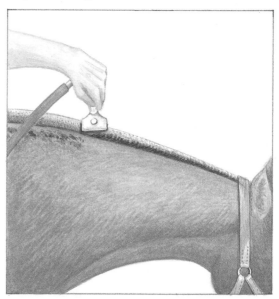

4. If the crest has wrinkles, finish like this. You will need a steady hand. The hogged mane should look even, with a straight edge on both sides.

Cutting or 'banging' a tail

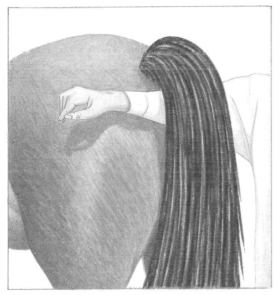

1. To avoid cutting the tail too short, and to cut at the correct angle, put your arm under the dock to raise the tail to the position it is in when the pony is moving.

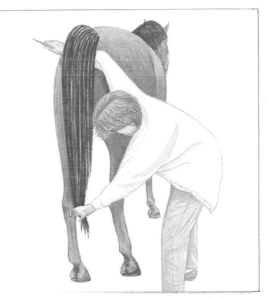

2. Supporting the dock with your right arm, measure the tail to the pony's chestnut. Use your left hand to mark the place and to hold the hairs at the correct angle.

3. Cut the tail straight across, or shape the end so that the centre hairs are slightly longer than the outside hairs. This may be difficult for small hands.

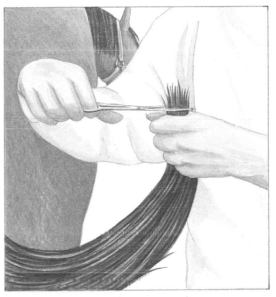

4. Repeat stage 2 and square off (or round off) any unlevel hairs to achieve a neat finish. The end will now lie parallel with the ground when the pony is moving.

Pulling a tail

Pulling the tail involves plucking out the side hairs and some of the hair from the centre of the top of the tail, to accentuate the shape and elegance of the dock

Advantages:
1   The tail always remains neat and tidy and does not need plaiting every time the pony goes to a show.
2   If the pony has rubbed his tail so that the hairs are too short to plait, pulling will make it look neat. Note that if the tail is rubbed badly the pony may need treatment for worms or a skin disorder, so consult your local vet.

Disadvantages:
1   A pulled tail affords less protection from the elements. Do not pull the tail of a pony who lives out of doors overnight in the winter.
2   Each week you will need to pull out enough hairs to keep the tail in shape.
3   If you want to grow the tail out, it will go through some untidy stages before looking normal again.

To achieve a good result, pull out more hairs from the edge of the dock than from the centre. Pull out the hairs a few at a time so that you do not leave 'holes'. You can always pull out more but you cannot put them back! The finished dock should look sleek and thin at the top before gradually widening into the fullness of the tail.

As with manes, the hairs will pull out more easily when the pony is warm. If the tail has not been pulled before take several days, working a little at a time to prevent soreness. Standing behind the pony to pull the tail can be dangerous. Beware of his kicking! If he is very sensitive stand to one side and ask someone to help you. When you have finished, brush the top of the tail with a water brush and put on a tail bandage. The bandage should not be left on overnight. To remove it, untie the tapes and slide it down the tail.

BEFORE

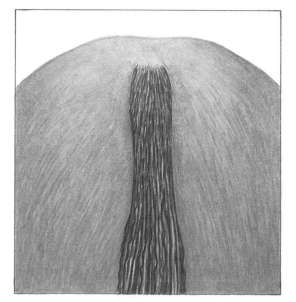

AFTER

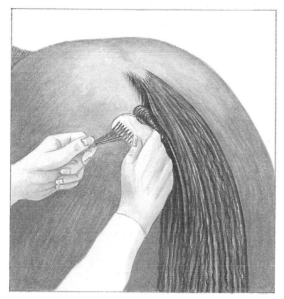

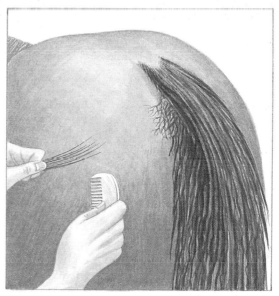

1. Brush the tail. Comb the hairs at the centre and sides of the dock. Comb a section of hair out from the edge. Grasp the longest hairs firmly and backcomb.

2. Pull out the hairs with a brisk jerk. The comb may be used to help. Repeat these two stages, working down in small sections. Stop half way down the dock.

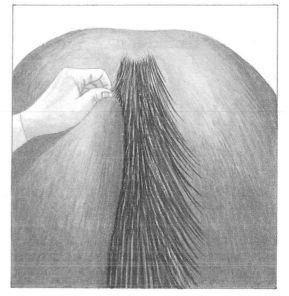

3. Comb, backcomb and pull out the centre hairs in the same way but pull less from the centre than from the sides. The dock should appear evenly covered with hair.

4. Pluck out any untidy hairs which remain. Then pull the other side of the dock so that both sides look the same. Finally, apply a tail bandage (see page 20).

Plaiting a tail Method 1

If the mane has been plaited it is correct for the tail to be either pulled or plaited. There is nothing quite as elegant as a well plaited (laced) tail, and although the braid looks complicated, it is quite easy to do.

The tail to be plaited must be:
1 In healthy condition, with long, thick hair growing from the top. A rubbed or pulled tail cannot be plaited.
2 Clean and well brushed out before you begin. (Note: Tail hairs break very easily, so when practising, always brush very gently with a soft brush: otherwise you will find after a while that there are no more hairs to plait!)

Secrets of good plaiting:
1 Dampen the hair well before beginning.
2 The tighter you make the plait at the top, the more secure the rest of the plait will be.
3 Plait the tail almost to the end of the dock, then continue with the single plait. Short plaits are not as elegant.

As soon as you have completed the plaiting, dampen the plait gently by patting it with a wet sponge. Then put on a tail bandage, carefully but firmly, to protect it. When it is time to remove the bandage, unwrap it gently. Sliding it off briskly would destroy the plait.

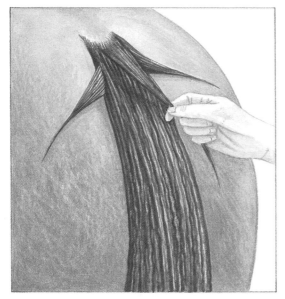

1. Brush out the tail. Comb and dampen the top. Isolate one bunch of hair from each edge, as high as possible, and one from the top of the centre of the dock.

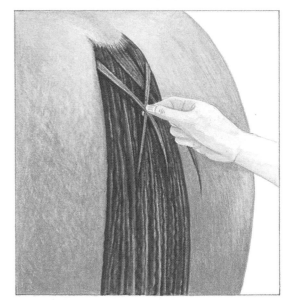

2. Begin to plait as on page 9 stage 2, but hold the plait in one hand, your thumb keeping it tight. Your free hand will add new bunches to the plait.

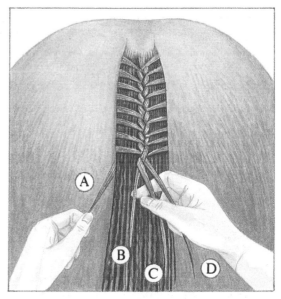

3. Isolate new bunches from the edge of the dock on alternate sides. Each bunch must be thin, so that the plait continues to be narrow and elegant.

4. Here new bunch A is prepared. B, C and D are segregated in the right hand. Join A and B. Hold them between middle and forefingers of the left hand.

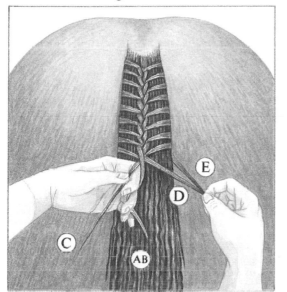

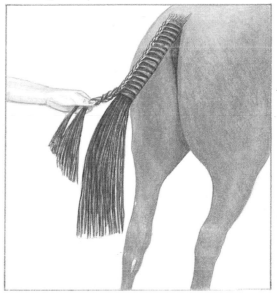

5. Swap C to left hand between middle and forefingers. New bunch E joins D, then AB goes over C into right hand. C now takes the same place as B in stage 4.

6. When you reach the end of the dock, stop adding bunches from the side, and continue with a simple plait to the end. (OR to 'Put up the tail' see page 23.)

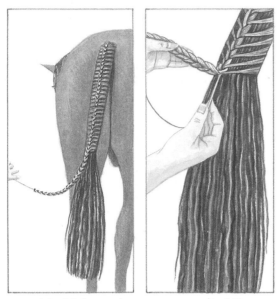

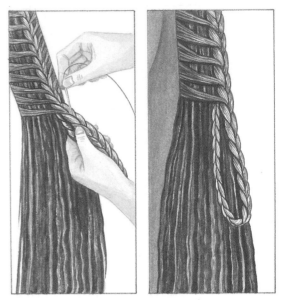

7 and 8. Make and secure a neat end by sewing, as shown in stages 3 and 4 on page 9. Sew the end up, tucked in above the dock and under the plait.

9 and 10. Sew down for a few inches to leave a smart loop. Finish off so that (a) the plait is secure, (b) the end of the plait does not show, and (c) there is no sign of thread.

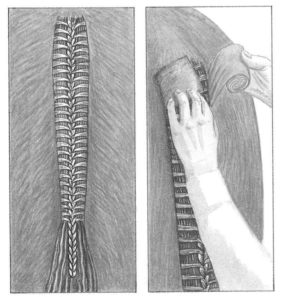

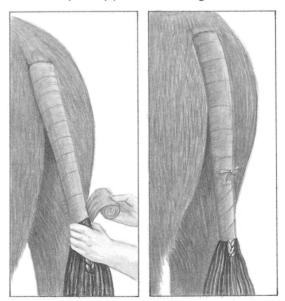

Putting on a tail bandage. Dampen the tail. Unroll a short piece of bandage. Put it under and round the tail as high as possible. Hold it in place and start bandaging tightly.

Continue almost to the end of the dock and then up again until you run out of bandage. Secure with a knotted bow. Bend the dock to its natural position.

Plaiting a tail Method 2

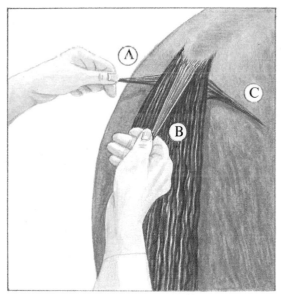

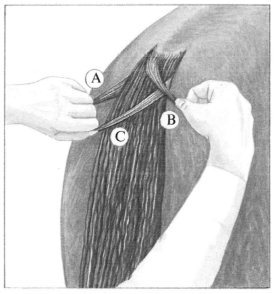

1. Here the plait will lie on the outside. Before you begin, practise plaiting, right under centre, left under centre. Then begin as for Method 1 on page 18.

2. Start to plait, C under B. A will then go under C, but it is easier first to select with your right hand a thin bunch of hair to form D.

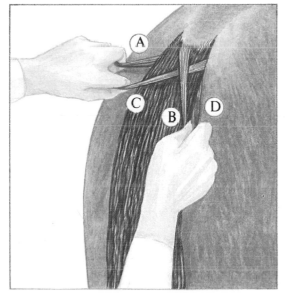

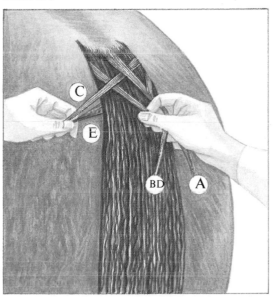

3. Join B to D. Then, holding BD between the middle and forefingers of your right hand, turn your left wrist and pass A under C into the right hand.

4. Select new bunch E to join C. Put CE between the middle and forefingers of the left hand. Turning your right wrist, pass BD under A into your left hand.

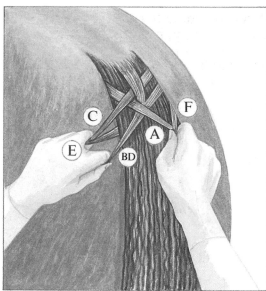

5. Select new bunch F to join A. Put AF between the middle and forefingers of the right hand. Turning your left wrist, pass CE under BD into your right hand.

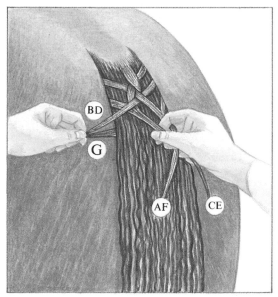

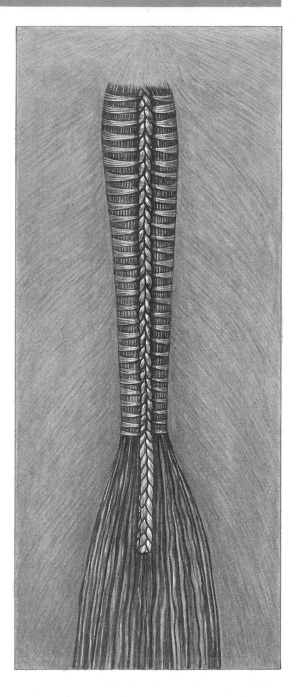

6. Select new bunch G to join BD. Continue as before to the end of the dock, plaiting tightly. To finish, see pages 19 (stage 4) and 20; or page 23.

Putting up a tail

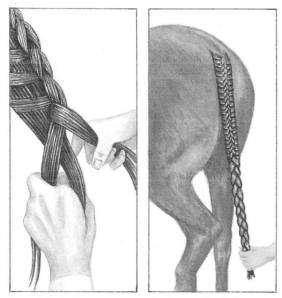

If you are going to be performing across country, hunting, or show jumping in muddy conditions it is useful to be able to 'put up' your pony's tail. Some ponies become irritated by the feel of a heavy muddy tail between their legs and may even kick at it, making them a danger to others. A put-up tail is more comfortable and will keep cleaner.

1 and 2. When you reach the end of the dock, divide the whole tail into 3 parts. Add one part to each of your 3 bunches and plait to the end of the tail

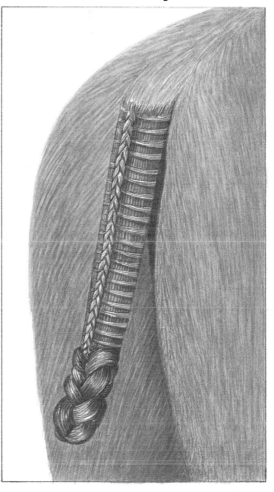

3 and 4. Secure it with a thick rubber band or by sewing. Roll it up under the dock and sew it up securely, on both sides of the dock. Take care not to prick the pony.

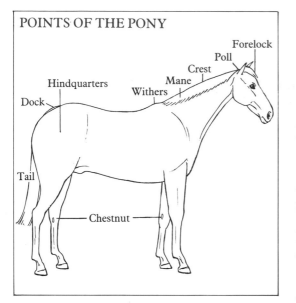

POINTS OF THE PONY

Forelock
Poll
Crest
Mane
Hindquarters
Withers
Dock
Tail
Chestnut

SAFETY CHECK LIST

- Work in a safe, peaceful place which is familiar to the pony: either a field, an enclosed yard, or a stable with good lighting.

- Remember to shut the gate or door.

- Tie the pony to breakable string attached to a strong ring or fence.

- Always beware of the pony kicking. Be careful where you stand.

- Wear rubber soles when clipping.

- Place the clipper cable where the pony cannot chew or tread on it.

- Never clip outside in wet conditions.

- Allow plenty of time. Most ponies fidget if they think you are hurried.

- Work in a quiet but purposeful way.

- Whatever happens, always keep calm.

EQUIPMENT NEEDED FOR EACH TASK

Headcollar and rope with clip.

Cutting a bridle path
Mane comb.
Scissors with rounded ends.

Pulling manes and tails
Small haynet to keep your pony amused.
Straw bales to go between you and the pony's hind legs when pulling tails.
Mane comb. Body brush. Water brush.
Thick rubber band to keep the mane out of the way if it is very long.
Tail bandage to put on pulled tails.
Water to damp tail before bandaging
If all else fails, a thinning comb.

Plaiting manes and tails
Small haynet.
Crate or box to stand on if necessary.
Half a bucket of water.
Body brush to brush mane and tail.
Water brush to dampen mane and tail.
Mane Comb. Damp sponge.
Setting lotion for flyaway hair.
Large needle with big eye.
Heavy-duty cotton from a saddler (the same colour as the mane or tail).
Scissors with rounded ends.
Rubber bands to match the pony's mane.
Tail bandage to protect plaited tails.

Hogging a mane
An experienced assistant to keep the pony still and to ensure that the clippers are adjusted correctly.
Box or crate to stand on if necessary.
Small haynet for pony.
Power point.
Clippers in good safe working order.
Extension cable.
Thin oil for clipping machine.
Oily rag and brush for clipper blades.
Body brush to brush away loose hair.